George Douglas Campbell Argyll

The Burdens of Belief and other Poems

George Douglas Campbell Argyll

The Burdens of Belief and other Poems

ISBN/EAN: 9783744717878

Printed in Europe, USA, Canada, Australia, Japan

Cover: Foto ©Thomas Meinert / pixelio.de

More available books at **www.hansebooks.com**

THE

BURDENS OF BELIEF

AND OTHER POEMS

BY THE

DUKE OF ARGYLL, K.G., K.T.

LONDON

JOHN MURRAY, ALBEMARLE STREET

1894

DEDICATORY PAGE

To EMILY, LADY TENNYSON, THIS VOLUME IS
DEDICATED BY THE AUTHOR, IN TOKEN OF A
LONG FRIENDSHIP, OF MANY HAPPY MEMORIES,
AND OF ONE GREAT SORROW.

INVERARAY: *November* 1893

PREFACE

LIKE MOST MEN who have spent many years in lite-
rary work of various kinds, I have occasionally, from
a very early age, amused myself by writing verse.
Having, however, a wholesome sense of the wide
spaces which may separate even verse which is fairly
good from verse which is genuine poetry, I have never
published more than a very few occasional contribu-
tions to periodicals of the day. The favourable
opinion, however, of some on whose taste and judg-
ment I can rely, encourages me to hope that lines
which have long given pleasure to a few may now
give pleasure also to at least a few more.

The principal composition in this volume has,
indeed, a more recent origin and a more serious purpose. It is an attempt to give some poetic form to
facts and suggestions connected with modern science
in its relations with religion and philosophy. Although

it is not to be admitted, even for a moment, that those relations are antagonistic, or that there is any tendency whatever in the physical sciences to bring about a divorce between the highest poetry and the highest philosophy, yet it cannot be denied that such an attempt as I have here made is beset with many difficulties, both in conception and in execution. The mere forms of logical reasoning are not poetic ; whilst the play of fancy and of imagination is liable to be bound and shackled by the strict language of physical conceptions. On the other hand, it is not less true that the progress of science in recent times has been singularly full of what may be called tran-scendental elements—full, that is to say, of suggested thoughts which go to establish in our minds the most fertile, perhaps, of all poetic conceptions—that, namely, of the Unity of Nature, and therefore of its manifold and inexhaustible relations with the human spirit. But as imagery is the very soul of poetry, it follows that every discovery enlarging our con-ceptions of the universe in which we live and of which we form an essential part, must, in the very nature of things, open out new vistas into those subtle and intimate analogies which give us the hidden meanings of the world. These are not only the province of the poet—they are his home. It is the highest function of his ' vision and faculty divine '

to see them, and to give to them some attractive
form and some melodious voice. All really great
poets have done this in some pre-eminent degree ;
and even such measures of shorter life as lesser men
have won, have been due to the same element,
however inferior in form or in power. This is a field
of thought in which I have long worked in other
forms of composition. But, thankful as I am for the
large acceptance which has attended two more
elaborate efforts in this direction, I know that it
affords but little presumption in favour of a transition
from the vehicle of prose to the vehicle of verse,
especially when the shortness of the poem has caused
a condensation both of thought and of expression
on which some most friendly critics have observed.
On the other hand, having the firmest confidence in
the steps of suggestion and of implied argument to
which expression has been given in these lines, I cast
them as seed upon the troubled waters of our time—
seed which may, or may not, be drifted to some
solitary shores where they may take root and grow.

The opening lines of 'The Burdens of Belief' are
intended to be a frank acknowledgment of the large
amount of truth which belongs to what is called the
agnostic aspects of the world. No man who seeks to
be quite honest with himself or just to others, can fail
to see those aspects, or ought to refrain from acknow-

ledging them. But it is an immense mistake to sup-
pose, as so many do, that those aspects of things have
been intensified or, still less, confirmed by the discoveries of modern science. The truth is that we are
all under an almost invincible temptation to exaggerate
beyond all reasonable bounds the extent to which
scientific discoveries have even touched, or affected
at all, the ultimate problems of humanity. The range
and effect of those discoveries upon the external con-
ditions of human life have indeed been so enormous—
the results of them in this lower range of work have
been so innumerable, and these results are at once
so astonishing and yet so pervading and familiar—that
we can hardly get rid of the impression that they must
have had some corresponding effects in the domain
of Thought. Yet nothing can be more certain, when
we come to examine this matter closely, than that
no such correspondence of effect does, or can, exist.
The ultimate problems of human life and thought are
like the 'Fixed Stars'—they have either no 'parallax,'
or, if any, such as can only be detected by observa-
tions of the utmost care and nicety. Just as with
the farthest stars their distance from us is so immense
that the whole of our earthly orbit shows in them
no apparent change of place, so, as regards all the
questions we most desire to ask and to solve in
philosophy and religion, they are almost wholly

unaffected by the utmost range of physical discovery.

And this arises mainly from a fact which has hardly been sufficiently observed—namely, that without one single exception no physical discovery of modern times has been really new in the ultimate principle or law upon which it depends, and which alone it can reveal. Not one of them has been anything more than some further application in detail of some principle or idea which, in the rough and in the large, had been long familiar to the human mind. This observation is true both of the discoveries of fact which have been the most purely physical and of the very transcendental conceptions which have been started by the sciences in the intellectual interpretation of them. Thus, for example, in the first of these two spheres of scientific activity, nothing, perhaps, strikes us more than the discovery of certain means or agencies whereby we can speak to other men with instantaneous velocity over all the continents of the globe. Yet the mechanical principle or law which is involved is nothing but an extension of the law by which our own vocal cords can communicate our thoughts across smaller distances by arbitrary signs conveyed through an intervening vibratory medium. The discovery and the yoking to our service of other media by which the same kind of contrivance can be worked through greater spaces, and with greater speed, involves no new principle whatever, and no new idea which even bears upon the greater problems of human thought. In like manner, the revelations of Astronomy in respect to the immensities of space are very impressive, but they fall infinitely short of that indelible impression on our own spirit which, in its conceptions, invests space not merely with a relative but with an absolute infinity. There is nothing new to us in conceiving of space as infinite. Chemistry, again, has gone perhaps nearer than any other of the physical sciences to introduce us to a *new* physical idea—that of chemical affinity, and its combinations. But some of the actual embodiments and exhibitions of chemical force—as in fire and in its uses—have been among the earliest facts known to man, and some of the earliest servants of his will. A yet more striking example of the same truth is to be found in perhaps the most recondite of modern discoveries—namely, those which connect all organic forms in one essential unity as regards the form and structure of the organic apparatuses which are the abodes of Life. There is nothing whatever in these discoveries which does not belong to one great, general, and obvious truth—which from time immemorial has been recognised—that in all animals there are a great number of strictly corresponding parts. The new discoveries are nothing but a confirmation and development of this familiar thought, and a series of proofs, wonderful indeed, that it runs true through the whole of nature, and is one of the most profound indications both of her methods and of her aims.

There is, however, one result of the latest discoveries of science which is well calculated to produce a really new and a very deep impression on our minds —a result which, however unexpected, is nevertheless in perfect harmony with all that was known to us before—I refer to the discoveries due to the spectrum analysis of light. Nothing, I think, which has ever been before accomplished, in the physical sciences, is to be compared with these discoveries in their bearing on speculative thought. They go far to prove the scientific truth of the old conception of the microcosm and the macrocosm—the conception that we are in ourselves an epitome of all that nature contains, and therefore that in new senses, as well as in the higher sense in which we had been told it before, the Kingdom of Heaven is within us. This is the fundamental conception which has been, however imperfectly and feebly, dwelt upon in the opening stanzas of the 'Burdens of Belief.' The vanity of expecting to find somewhere—far away— the truths which really lie within us and around us :

the identity in their ultimate nature of that which we call Instinct with that which we call Inspiration ; the reasonableness of the idea of an Incarnation ; the perfect naturalness and consequent credibility of strictly predictive prophecy—these and other kindred conceptions are the animating ideas of this poem, as ideas which all find their best and their only solution in Christian Belief.

The lines on the funeral of Tennyson were written under a painful impression of the total omission, or the very inadequate recognition, in many other obituary verses, of the noble religious and ethical character—the 'splendid purpose'—of the great Laureate's writings. I should hardly have ventured to present them to the public as even an approach to the tribute which is due to Tennyson on the most majestic aspects of his poetry, had it not been that they have been kindly accepted as such by her to whom this little volume is dedicated, and to whom the concluding words of these lines refer : words spoken of her to me—not long ago—by her illustrious husband.

CONTENTS

THE BURDENS OF BELIEF

I

SILENCE :—as if 'twere heard
   In this low darkened world of ours ;
The absence of one spoken word
   Through all our waiting hours ;
'Tis this that wakes our cry,—
   The weary, vanquished, cry to hear
Some voices speaking from on high,
   Some help to draw us near
To Nature's living soul,
   And from her sealèd lips to draw
The secret of her mystic scroll
   Of order and of Law.

II

Responding as she may
  To him who, digging, deeply delves
She leaves us, but at close of day,
  Some shadow of ourselves.
A vaster shadow? Yes ;
  But still we seek some nobler thing,
For something that can raise and bless,
  Some vision of the King.

III

Yet farthest realms of space
  In which our largest units die [1]
Have sent us nought that we can trace
  That is not also nigh.
Orion's stars that burn,
  With furious heat, in glowing flame,
Hold nought but elements that turn
  Into our flesh and frame.

[1] Note I., Appendix.

No words of Nature teach,
  However far they bear us hence,
That we can soar beyond the reach
  Of matter and of sense.

IV

Even the blessèd light,
  Lest we should love it over-much,
Stands now revealed to mental sight
  As being only touch,
Through something interposed
    'Twixt Orb and Orb, and ever on,
Until our wearied wings are closed
    In effort spent and gone,
To think or to conceive
  What that fine air of worlds can be
That brings us all that we receive
  Out of its ocean sea.
In it our globe was born,
  The myriad globes that round it shine,
And other globes from others torn,
  The eldest births of Time.

V

And then—at least perhaps—[1]
Through it the power that Newton saw
Which every other overlaps—
    The universal law
    That holds the worlds in place,—
Works in its own mysterious way
Through all illimitable space,
    The fountain of our day.
Nor brings it light alone,—
    This largest, strongest thing we know ;
It shapes the gem within the stone,
    The crystals in the snow.
It breathes through all the earth,
    Lending its atoms mystic power ;
Giving alike the thunder birth,
    And petals to the flower.

VI

So turn we home once more
    From distant quest for what is near,

[1] Note II., Appendix.

Nor lives alone on farther shore,
　　But veiled beside us here.
Beside, and deep within—
　　Within this living soul·of·ours
Most veiled of all, yet next of kin
　　To the everlasting Powers :
Born of great Nature's blood,
　　Flesh of its flesh, and bone of bone,
Most nearly must it once have stood
　　Close to the central Throne ;
For still through time and space
　　No voice there seems unknown on earth,
No meaning look on her vast face
　　That is of alien birth.
As tissues fairy-fine
　　In creature-eyes prepared for sight
Catch sister waves in radiant line,
　　Transfigured into light,
So in the realms of thought
　　Fresh secrets flash from out the whole,
From age to age new knowledge brought
　　With whispers to the soul :

And blest the voice profound
That of our home so speaketh well,
Of treasures that may there be found,
The House wherein we dwell.

VII

The work of Mind we know,—
The spirit-work that is our own ;
Our thoughts of Matter come and go
In wanderings alone,
Dissolving in the light
Of Spirit when it thinks and sees,
Brute Matter, whether here in sight
Or in the Pleiades,
Is only as the clay
That yieldeth well to potter's hand.
And takes some form, as told it may,
In fittest shapes to stand ;
By some strange virtue brought,
Some tie to us unknown in kind,
To incarnate the powers of thought,
And be the home of Mind.

VIII

Unknown,—but this we know,   `
    The mode of work is like our own ;
Material things are moulded so ;
    'Tis not pure Will alone.
Through ages now revealed,
    Since wandering atoms clashed in fire,
We see the footprints, long concealed,
    That led from low to higher.
Making for ends foreseen,
    Beyond all summits we can climb,
The grand creative steps have been
    By means prepared in Time.

IX

Close veiled some truths may be
    In common things from sightless eyes,
Which rarer forms can let us see
    And make the blinded wise.
Low beasts that swim and take
    Their prey on ocean's sands and weed,

Now wield the power whose shocks can break
   The oak-tree like a reed.
Through ages long ago,
   The fibres of their living frame
Began to bend, entwining so
   That, silent, rose and came
A wondrous organ, made
   Of plates, and cups, and nervèd cells,
To store and launch through channels laid,
   The mighty Force that dwells,—
Unseen, unfelt, in us,—
   In earth and sea, in sun and space,
Yet voiceless save where gathered thus,
   Or in the storm-cloud's face.[1]

X

One cause—the future known ;
   This only key unlocks the gate :
We see blind Matter backward thrown ;
   Forces on Purpose wait.

[1] Note III., Appendix.

Before their work began
　All creature-organs slowly grew ;
Foreseeing ever held the van
　In wings before they flew.[1]
In meaner forms of clay,
　Through stages of a long ascent,
Some little breakings of our day
　To living things were lent.
By method and by plan,
　Which in dim outline we can see,
Fit organs are built up in man
　For functions yet to be.

XI

Fit—yes : but for what task ?
　'Tis here, alas, the clouds close in,
Shrouding the questions we would ask,
　In horrid shapes of sin.
All other creatures play
　Their native parts in perfect tune,
As myriad beings sing their way
　Through all the suns of June.

[1] Note IV., Appendix.

Between their joy of life,
    And strength to them by nature given,
Between their armour and their strife
    No rent or break is riven.
Strange inborn instincts lead
    The secret weapons of Design,
In wielding powers to meet their need
    Far down a distant line.

XII

The armèd fly that calls
    On oak or rose to nurse her young,
Sees them build up the cradle' walls,
    On balmy branches hung.
No babe or child of man
    In such a fragrant cot is laid ;
No tree or bush so lends the plan
    Of its own sun and shade
To hold an alien birth,
    And out of its fair tissues make
The closest, tenderest home on earth
    For his high being's sake.

Yet 'tis for stranger's sake,
   Not for its own, the home is made ;
The walls its vital juices take,
   Its flowers aside are laid.
Such far off purpose lives
   Not in low worm or insect-hour,
She knows not what it is that gives
   Her own mysterious power.[1]

XIII

Australia's bird that lays
   Her beauteous eggs in hatching-mound,
Nor sits, like other birds, her Days,
   But leaves them in the ground :
Born heirs of their own land,
   Her young, full-armed to fly and run,
Open their eyes from coral sand
   As if they knew the sun.[2]
The Bee that seals her cell,
   The prism'd cell that she has made,—

[1] Note V., Appendix.
[2] Note VI., Appendix.

Unconscious trust, and faith as well
    Has with her treasures laid.

XIV

Desires to Nature true
    Are what we hear and see alone,—
Desires that with the creature grew
    Most true where least is known.
'Tis Inspiration seen ;
    The most all-present thing on earth,
In all degrees it must have been
    Re-born with every birth.
All creatures know, untold,
    The working of their gifted powers ;
All living germs must first infold
    The promise of their flowers.

XV

'Tis here our wondering cries
    Ask why fair Nature's noblest child
Sees no such guide, but errs and dies,
    In wanderings fierce and wild ?
Inventing curse and pain
    For self and all that breathe around,

The useless slayer and the slain,
  Man mingles with the ground.
Dark imaged in desires
  And vices which are his alone,
Some God he forges in his fires
  Or shapes from wood and stone ;
Then devil-whispers come,
  Dark and more dark suggestions rise,
Some foul and hideous, thirsty some
  For victim-blood and cries.
Whole continents of Earth,
  Most blest in every flower and clime,
Have lain beneath this monstrous birth
  Through agonies of time.
No power redeeming seen,
  No broadening streaks of rising day,
But dens of beasts where men have been,
  And cities swept away.

XVI

Out of these deeps we cry ;
  The Why, the How, we long to know :

Faint gleams of light will flicker by,
That, breaking, come and go.
One thing, indeed, we see,—
That good is good, and ill is ill ;
That evil must for ever be
Fountain of evil still.
Thus in the heart of things
Some deeper law is working right,
On sin a blacker shadow flings
And goodness crowns with light.
So out of darkness rise
Some glad suggestions of a Cause,
Some grateful vision greets our eyes
Of just and righteous laws.

XVII

The highest things we know
Are conscious faith, and trust, and love ;
But needs with these must Freedom go,
And willing hearts must move.
True faith can only live
Where some One is believed and known,—

Freedom to give or not to give
   The love that is our own.
Not as the beasts fulfil
   Their own small being's law,
Willing, as by directed Will,
   Doing as if they saw :—
In this they speak one word,—
   A word that most we need to hear,
Pointing to one eternal law,
   Which reigns supremely here :—
In them no power is planted,
   No born desire in them is shown
Save where some fitting joy is granted
   Perfect attainment known.

XVIII

In man the inner fires,
   That give his noblest souls their tone,
Live only in unquenched desires :
   In this he stands alone.
Alone : but only then
   If nothing can his nature meet,

And if the noblest thoughts of men
Wander with homeless feet.
But then—in Nature stands
Nothing that holds such lonely place ;
'Gainst this she speaks through all her lands
With one true steadfast face.
One in her deepest thought,
True to One Mind in all her plan,
She of her inmost treasures wrought
Her noblest creature—Man.
Her crowning work : not there
Can false, untrue, alone prevail,—
Not in that promise proud and fair
Her strong foundations fail.

XIX

But in the gifts that raise
Man's eyelids to another morn,
That make him look to endless days
Yet leave him so forlorn,
Are powers of heart and will
That make him free to choose his way—

To choose the good, to choose the ill,
  The darkness for the day :
For in that highest part
  Of higher things he hopes to see,
A wise and understanding heart
  His only guide can be.
'Give me thine heart,' Love asks,
  This is the only word she speaks,
Free given—not in appointed tasks—
  This the response she seeks.
And so one truth we reach,—
  High voices that within us call,
Although they draw, persuade, and teach,
  Must leave us free to fall.

XX

Is this a word that shakes,—
  Ah, how can we endure that 'must'?
Some limit the Almighty takes ;
  Some limit, then, to trust?
No : for all trust reposes
  On things our souls cannot deny ;

C

Thus, in ourselves, our search discloses
 Some One who cannot lie ;—
Some One whose changeless laws,
 No burden that we bear alone,
But guiding th' Universal Cause
 Since they are all His own.
And so, the 'needs must be,'—
 That 'must' of the Eternal Will,—
Is strongest stay that we can see,—
 His Truth and Mercy still.

XXI

No light—no voice—we say ?
 In saying this can we forget
' If thou hadst known in this thy day,'
 That voice from Olivet ?
Too near : Is this the cry ?
 Too close to us to be divine :
No signs that flash from out the sky,
 Mere words from Palestine ?
Ask we some distant sphere ?
 Are we so blind as reason thus :—

His mother and His brethren here,
　Were they not all with us?
Ay! More than this to strain
　Our faith in all the path He trod,
If we can't hear except with pain
　How near to us is God.

XXII

Born in a low estate,
　Nursed in a poor Judean town,
Journeying from its humble gate,
　Unarmed with least renown;
Nowhere to lay His head,
　With nothing that He called His own,
Seeking the Desert's stony bed
　That He might pray alone;
Walking in common day,
　Living among the very least,
Speaking with voice not far away,
　Sitting at marriage feast;
Upon Tiberias' Sea,
　Watching the draught of fisher's net,

Choosing from such his friends to be
Beside Gennesaret.

XXIII

Perhaps more hard for those
Who saw how thus He lived on earth—
Even for them He loved and chose,
To see His Heavenly Birth—
Than 'tis for us who know
How all His words recorded then,
Over the world have triumphed so,
And been the Light of Men ;
That worn-out world that lay
Around Him as He stood unknown,
With all its frame has passed away,
And left His face alone.

XXIV

All thoughts not passed indeed,
For heathen souls had felt their way
To visions that still hold the meed
Of our best love to-day ;—

Yet powerless over Man
   To fix his vagrant mind to act,
As nothing ever will or can
   Save Truth revealed as fact.
Our most aspiring wings
   With nothing to sustain their flight,
Flutter mid unsubstantial things,
   And broken tracks of light.

XXV

Yet failed no child of man
   To hold in all his dreamings wild
Some lines of guidance from the plan
   Of one primeval child.
The roots of right lay deep ;
   Within his heart of hearts he saw
The duty of his Will to keep
   True to some binding law.
Not in his darkest time
   Unknown to him the words ' I ought.'
Its steeps of knowledge still to climb,
   His sorest travail wrought.

It was to such He came,
To soul-wide longings He appealed,
To raise and meet the smouldering flame
In many hearts revealed.

XXVI

Transfiguring all of good,
This world in human hearts had seen,
Yet at the bar of Rome he stood
Despised as Nazarene ;
Such plea in common way,
As might from day to day arise,—
No Jew or Roman saw that day
What passed before his eyes ;
They saw a humble One,
With gentle mien and sorrowed brow
Accused of scorning Cæsar's throne—
Where are the Cæsars now ?
Herod and Pilate—nought ;
Opprobrious sounds in human ear,—
The nameless One before them brought
Mankind bows down to hear.

XXVII

Then—whence those words of light,
　　Those prophet-words that pierce the gloom ?
' Servant, in whom is my delight,
　　I called thee from the womb.'
' My sorrow spent in vain,
　　Israel will not learn of me.'
' Yea, through thy sorrow and thy pain,
　　Thou'lt triumph gloriously.'
' Rejected and abhorred
　　By those to whom I showed the way ;
Yet Kings shall see thee as their Lord
　　In rising of thy day.'
' Not o'er that narrow land
　　Between the Jordan and the sea,
Kept in the hollow of My hand
　　Thy power and might shall be.'
' Little for thee to hold
　　Proud Judah's stubborn tribes alone,
Far ends of earth within thy fold,
　　These shall be yet thine own.'

'On all the shores where throng

The sons of Japhet, Shem, or Ham

Shall fall the blessings that belong

To seed of Abraham.'[1]

XXVIII

Came these strange words from Jew?

Who led that spirit-path he trod?

Whence came that mystic vision true

To child of Jacob's God?

So fiercely tribal—nursed

In scorn 'gainst other nations hurled,

How brought to see in those accursed

God's heirs—a heathen world?

And yet to whom apply

Such vision and its words, alone,

Save to that One—how pass Him by—

Whom now the Gentiles own?

Like rain on thirsty ground,

Like morning dew on tender grass,

So did His sayings fall around,

And o'er the nations pass.

[1] Note VII., Appendix.

Most distant Isles of Sea,
  As in old vision Prophets saw
Have His disciples come to be
  And waited on His law.

XXIX

Nor His the Past alone ;
  For every gain that we can get
Comes from the seed that He has sown,
  Less than half-fruited yet ;
Oft choked in weedy soil,
  Unless full well it tended be ;
Men mock the travail and the toil
  He spent in Galilee.
An unexhausted store,
  River of Life too full to dry,
Fountain of truth yet more and more
  For all who live or die.
Wrested—misunderstood—
  His words have oft been turned to ill,
Yet ever all new forms of good
  Seen as His holy Will.

XXX

Outshining all the ways—
The little ways that we have run—
His laws alone can perfect days
That we have scarce begun.
By no suspended laws,
Confusion on our nature cast,
But in His words, though many a pause,
His love revealed at last.
Not by some wayward Will,
But one calm Will that changeth not,
And works to teach, rebuke, fulfil,
Are His sure triumphs wrought.
No signs He gave of power
To heal and cure all human pain,
Not even that supremest hour
That woke the Child of Nain,
With such strong witness speak
To all He is, through grief and strife,
For them who grope, yet faithful seek
The Way, the Truth, the Life.

XXXI

An Incarnation : no?
    Is this a thought too hard to hold?
In lower forms it must be so,
    A thousand times retold.
Not as in our Design
    The maker stands outside his fires ;
In Nature, the creator's sign,
    Unseen, within, He moves—inspires.[1]
Spirit—of all the sum,
    Breathing through all that we can scan—
Most nearly does that Spirit come
    Within the mind of man.
If that were only pure,
    Its God-like gifts unbroken,
How might its beauty then endure,
    Of life, and love, the token.

XXXII

Not all explained? Ah, no :
    Some deeper mysteries even shown,

[1] Note VIII., Appendix.

A fellow-feeling with our woe

In One beside the Throne.

Evil—as ever dark ?

Ay,—darker than it seemed before ;

Some war in Nature's self,—yet hark !

Songs from a farther shore ?

Nor from that shore alone ;

For even here dread sins can cease,—

The bad are changed—repentance known—

Past understanding, Peace.

As with new life imbued,

Such the Imperial power that's given,

' All things unto Himself subdued,'

This is the hope of heaven :—

A light so self-revealing

That they who patient wait may see

The silent wings that carry healing

To all the wounds that be.

XXXIII

Not yet all things put under :—

Some evil Form still holds the strife

That can the gift from promise sunder,
   The Way, the Truth, from life.
Yet here His strength is shown ;
   On neck of foes His feet are set,
Slow-mounting the Eternal Throne,
   Where He will triumph yet.
Within this world, a world :
   We see the heart and soul of things :
Foul idols from their temples hurl'd
   Beneath one King of kings.
And yet no thunder stroke,
   But still small voice we hear,
As if our own first nature spoke,
   Higher, yet closely near.
And so its words repeat
   The note that our impatience jars,
The only light that lights our feet
   Is—like the light of stars—
Not something strange or new
   To all that we have known on Earth,
But nearest things revealed to view
   As through a second birth.

XXXIV

Those baffled powers we feel,—
How weak, how strong, we hardly know ;
Barred in as if with bars of steel,
Now see these burst and go ;
No longer what they seemed,
A hopeless rift in Nature's plan,
Those powers by Son of God redeemed,
Because, too, Son of Man.
As fellow-soldiers they,
To bear one only standard on,
Hear the loud bugle for each day,
Until the fight be won.
Of His great army part,
Not now perplexed, in action dumb,
They rise new-nerved in mind and heart
To make His Kingdom come.

XXXV

For such is His domain,
So closely near, so everywhere,

All faithful hands can sow some grain,
  And bring some seed to bear.
As in a land of lakes
  Deep-valleyed with a thousand rills,
The mighty pulse of ocean makes
  Far home among the hills,
And every fisher's boat,
  In wooded creek with smoke up-curled,[1]
Still rests upon the seas that float
  And circle round the world,—
So does God's Kingdom wind
  Its arms beneath all ways of men ;
Far wandering sails of human kind
  Can be turned home again.

XXXVI

Sometimes one living soul,
  On fire with love of love, and truth,
New touched as with a living coal,
  Mailed in immortal youth,
Can wield some sword of heaven,
  Can smite with one great stroke for men

[1] Note IX., Appendix.

Some idol shrine, some demon-leaven
    That will not curse again.
Not less the bended knees
    Of humbler work accepted be,
'Given unto the least of these,
    They're given unto Me.'
Full oft in lonely path
    Of human life, and sin and sorrow,
We see the power His Spirit hath
    To make of night the morrow.
From each afflicted face,
    Scarce raised by faith above the ground
There stream the rays of heavenly grace,
    Shedding its peace around.

XXXVII

Mysteries unsolved ?   Ah, yes ;
    Òf these our cup is full to brim ;
Yet light enough to guide and bless,
    Enough to follow Him.
No hard enigmas fall ;
    No darkest doubt dissolves in flame,

To those who will not hear His call ;
  There is no other Name.
None other sheds one ray,
  One single ray of living light,
To strike this world and chase away
  The darkness of its night.

XXXVIII

When most we try through pain,
  Some battle with the sense of sin,
Most do His words return again—
  'My Kingdom is within.'
Eternal truth ; 'tis so ;
  Nor less these other words of His :
Supremest hope that we can know
  To 'see Him as He is.'

THE
BURIAL OF ALFRED, LORD TENNYSON,
IN WESTMINSTER ABBEY

October 12th, 1892

PROPHET and Bard, whose every word
 Will be the home, through coming years,
Of all who speak this English tongue
 In life and joy, in death and tears.

We lay thee in our sorrow down,
 Remembering all that thou hast said
Of those who hold, in seeming sleep,
 The vaster knowledge of the dead.

In daring yet in reverent thought,
 Unbound by forms which others need,
Thine eyes were fixed with longing gaze
 On Him Who is the 'Life indeed.'

'Strong Son of God, Immortal Love,'
Are words which came from out thine heart.
We feel them breathing through thy song
        In all its melodies of Art.

The mysteries of the world to thee
        In all its present, all its past,
Dissolved in one undying faith
        That 'Love will conquer at the last.'

And Love was pure in all thy Verse,
        The love of friendship early drawn
To noble manhood in its youth,
        And genius in its golden dawn.

And when thou speak'st the love of loves,
        The bridal love of human life,
The morning bells of marriage peal
        O'er perfect woman, perfect wife.

Nor less do baseness, hate and scorn,[1]
        Stand withered in thy scathing eyes :
Then touched to penitence by thee,
        We see the trembling souls arise.

[1] Note X., Appendix.

Repentance and the power of prayer
  Were never sung as sung by thee ;
The stricken form of Guinevere
  Their type till time shall cease to be.

No voice so strong to spread your fame,
  Heroic deeds, recorded here,
No voice so tender or so true
  For those who stand around the bier.

And when the gate of science throws
  Too wide her door to guesses wild,
No tones like thine may call them back
  To wisdom as the elder child.

And yet no spirit felt as thine
  The prison bars that close us round ;
And when true knowledge seemed to speak
  No head so bent to catch her sound.

The ocean of that inner life
  'Cross which there gleams some passing sail,
Seemed ever murmuring in thine ear
  ' Behind the Veil, behind the Veil.'

And yet to thee how thin that Veil ;
That life how present in its power ;
Suffused by all thy magic words
Through earth and sea, through sun and shower.

No bud is opened in the Spring,
No banner of a leaf unfurled,
That does not wake, in thy response,
Some hidden meanings of the world.

All this round earth is home to thee,
In all its seas of storm and calm,
From where the iceberg thunders shock
To ripples underneath the palm.

The blinding blaze of tropic climes,
Flooding the eastern sky with light,
Dense forests silent in the heat,
The sudden falling of the night.

And in the lands of ancient fame,
No painter's touch so true as thine,
To trace the landscape of the past,
The laurelled shores of corn and wine.

But chiefly in this Island home,
    Where seasons change with silent feet,
Where Autumn leaves are slow to fall,
And Winter with his snow and sleet

Gives place ere yet the year has turned
    To one pale flower, whose coming tells
That Spring has wakened underground
    And warbles in her snowdrop bells.

There is no charm unmarked by thee
    In all this sea-girt land of ours,
No shadow thrown by 'foliaged elms'
    On resting kine 'mid summer flowers.

The village church embowered in trees,
    With old grey tower or pointed spire,
Calling to prayer, has woke from thee
    The deepest measures of thy lyre.

The 'bushless pike,' the naked down,
    The waters trenched across the plain
From sky to sky, till windy dune .
    Takes all their tribute to the main.

And when the great Atlantic clouds
Roll eastward in their 'wild unrest,'
No glassy pool reflects so true
The gorgeous tumult of our West ;

The moated grange, the miller's wheel,
The cottage roses of our birth,
The forest glades of hyacinth
'Like heaven up-breaking through the earth ;'

And all to perfect music set,
In tones as sweet as silver bells,
Or those dear notes in which the Thrush
His love to quiet woodland tells.

They say the Poet's Art can live
In beauteous Form alone, forsooth ;
Thou sayest in thy nobler voice
That Beauty is the child of Truth.

Dear Friend, the Friend of forty years,
Of gentle strength and nameless grace,
I join with thee in this sad heart
One 'tender spiritual face.' [1]

[1] Note XI., Appendix.

TO THE LAUREATE

ON HEARING HIM READ THE PROOF-SHEETS OF
THE 'IDYLLS OF THE KING,' 1857

I HEAR the voice whose organ tones
 Will sound through Time for ever,
While mourning hearts still live in love
 That Death has failed to sever ;—
Strong human voice, deep, tender, true
 To every mood of sorrow,
To broken accents round the grave,
 And to the calmer morrow ;
To blessèd memories of the dead :
 To converse pure and high
In fruitful gardens of the soul
 'Mid blooms that cannot die ;
To clouds that gather in the dark,
 Then break with flash and thunder
In rending strokes that leave us mute ;
 The mystery and the wonder
That wait on death. All chords are thine :
 They tremble under thee.
Oh ! sound again to soothe and bless
 Sad souls that are to be.

OUR DEAD

SOMETIMES I think that those we've lost,
Safe lying on th' Eternal Breast,
Can hear no sounds from earth that mar
The perfect sweetness of their rest ;
But when one thought of holy love
Is stirred in hearts they love below,
Through some fine waves of ambient air,
They feel, they see it, and they know.
As rays unseen—abysmal light—
Are caught by films of silver salt
When these are set to watch by night
The wheelings of the starry vault,—
So may the souls that live and dwell
In one great soul, the Fount of all,
Feel faintest tremblings in the sphere
On which such footsteps gently fall.
No evil seen, no murmurs heard,
No fear of sin, or coming loss,
They wait in light, imperfect yet,
The final triumphs of the Cross.

THE TWO CLOUDS

Two clouds, slow drifting in the blue,
  Passed overhead one summer day ;
Their paths seemed diverse to my view,
  As either floated on its way.

I watched to see them—how they'd meet
  And how they'd battle in the sky :
They battled not, but seemed to greet
  And hail each other from on high.

And then I saw how crystal deeps
  Had failed to teach my human sight
The spacious bounds our planet keeps
  Within her gleaming halls of light.

The paths, which seemed of diverse birth,
  The same soft breath of air had given :
Only, one cloud was nearer earth,
  The sister-cloud was nearer heaven.

The movements of the way below
But seemed to cròss the way above ;
As diverse workings fail to show
The counsels of eternal love.

Danbury, *June* 8, 1892

A MOTE

ON one fair autumn morn the sunbeams smote
Through creviced inlets on my darkened room,
And in their rays the sudden-silvered mote
Flashed out, and quickly lost itself in gloom :

Fit emblem this of all our human path ;
From dark it passeth into dark again ;
Such fleeting course it is our spirit hath,
So pass between two darks the lives of men.

Yet as the mote, unseen, floats ever on,
And yieldeth not its substance into nought,
So of our mind, when outward form is gone
It loseth not the essence which it brought.

If that which we call matter never dies,
    Enduring ever though transfused in forms,
Can this great thing that so self-conscious lies
    Melt more to nothing than the dust of storms?

No thing so self-existent as a mind,
    So single, or so rounded as a whole,
The thinking power that is in human kind,
    The power, within, we know of as the soul.

And as the mote that floats in viewless ways
    Shines with a brilliance that is not its own,
So does our living soul reflect the rays
    Of one great Life that is to us unknown.

Yet something is there in our inner grain
    Which feels the light that on itself is thrown,
Feels it as light, nor feels it all in vain,
    For it can gaze, and love, till more is shown.

And more must come when souls recross the Dark,
    And wake again in splendours whence they came ;
When life no longer, here, a slender spark,
    But there—unquenched, beholds the central Flame

From whence have come all longings for the Truth,
And all desires for fuller life of love
For life unbroken—some undying youth,—
That sees—and needs not to believe, or prove.

———

TO A BUST OF
SLEEP—POPPY-WREATHED

BEQUEATHED BY HARRIET HOWARD, SECOND
DUCHESS OF SUTHERLAND

I

THOSE eyes so calmly closed in rest,
  Beneath sweet Sleep's memorial flower,
  Are eyes that wake in me the power
Of all we have the first and best,—
The power that brings us back, to-day,
  Those joys of life that have been cast
  In moulded memories of the past,
Where Time has rested on his way.

Pale marble form, upon whose brow
  The poppy wreath droops down in peace,
  Emblem of hours when troubles cease,
As mine with thee are silent now,
Thou stood'st beside the bed of one
  To whom a blessèd child was born :
  She saw thee first in summer morn ;
She saw thee when the day was done.

II

Now all that day comes back to me ;
  The sense of beauty, love of Art,
  The overflowings of a heart
That bled for all the ills that be :
The flashing eye, the nostril wide,
  When tale of wrong but reached her ear :
  For suffering seen—the quickest tear
That ever fell by woman's side :
And when harsh judgments of the world
  In clamour drowned the voice of truth,
  In all men's sight she held for ruth,
And banners of Belief unfurled.[1]

[1] Note XII., Appendix.

Hoping all things, believing all,
  Where noble nature seemed to rest,
  Nor less within her kindred breast
Where steps of genius seemed to fall.

III

Then when that land whose beauty's spell
  Such hapless gift had proved to be,
  Sent forth the man who set it free,
She hailed the Voice of England well.
Once more, when came across the wave
  One lonely woman's piercing cry
  That shook men's conscience from on high
And broke the fetters of the slave,
Her arms—how stretched they wide to greet
  The soul that breathed, the hand that wrote,
  The slender form that blew that note,
And cast our garlands at her feet ! [1]

IV

How charmed by her the wise and good,
  How beamed on them her radiant eye !
  To her no baseness dared come nigh,
Abashed all forms of envy stood.

[1] Note XIII., Appendix.

No tone of vice could she endure ;
   In her great presence roughness fell ;
   The light and reckless owned her spell,
And for a while the coarse were pure.
Full oft I've seen the doubtful jest
   Rise to the lips of some whose walk
   Lay in the paths of careless talk,
Then sink beneath her glance, repressed.

V

Quick as her eyes with light divine
   In catching beauty interfused,
   To see the tints of life confused,
They were as gently closed as thine.
And then to me when I had won
   Of those she bore the first and best,
   How have I felt the home, the rest,
The love she gave me as a son.
Sleep on—fair marble bust of Sleep :—
   Your fallen lids for me enclose
   More tender perfumes than the rose,
And fount of tears too calm to weep.

LINES TO E. C. G. ON HIS
MOTHER'S DEATH

March 30, 1892

I

You'VE lost your Mother : happy friend,
 Since you so long have loved her well,
 And only now you hear the bell
That tolls a long awaited end.
But I who never knew that love—
 The love to her that bore me due —
 Can only keep my fancy true
By flights, as of a homing dove,
To memories that are almost lost
 In the dim light of infant years,—
 To one faint image that appears
As pale and silent as a ghost.
One flower she loved, some souls that drew
 The boundless homage of her youth ;
 Some wingèd seeds from fields of Truth
That lighted on her mind and grew—

All these have reached me from the past,
　　As precious things are wafted o'er
　　The seas that fetch from shore to shore,
And bring them to our feet at last.

II

A few dim records of those years,
　　When she was full of life and joy,
　　Alone have crossed me since a boy,
And left me with imagined tears.
Yet often in the crowd of life,
　　And 'midst some voices of applause,
　　And in some pecking of the daws,
And in the battle and the strife,
I've wondered if from out that brow
　　Her eyes were set on me and mine,
　　As hers were set on thee and thine,
For whom these bells are tolling now ;
That brow of which the painter's art
　　Has made the gentle lines to rise
　　Above the arch of tender eyes
That look me through from heart to heart.

III

Yet vainly thus we try to hold
  The place well filled by voice and sight,
  The touch, the memories, and the light
Of dear communion with the Old.
And so be comforted, my friend,
  For thou hast had from dawn of day
  A Mother's love to gild thy way
A life-long sonship to the end.
And thou canst hear her voice for aye ;
  And thou canst see her stately mien ;
  All lives for thee that e'er has been,
Till thine own years have passed away.
Most blest of all—the part was thine
  To speak the words, ' Remember me, —
  To give to her,—'twas granted thee,—
The Sacred Bread, the Sacred Wine ;
And, in communion with her Lord,
  To see her breathe her latest breath,
  To see her close her eyes in death,
And open on the Living Word.

What wouldst thou more ?   The very best
Is spoken by that passing bell—
To thee, dear friend, it speaketh well,
And only of accomplished rest.

ON OPENING A PREHISTORIC TOMB

1892

(IN ROSS OF MULL, NEAR IONA)

I

WHEN wert thou, brother, laid
In this thy wild yet careful grave,
Midst rocky forms by surges made
Of some old Ocean wave?
Perchance thine eyes could hail,
Coming from far across the main,
The bark that bore with blessèd sail
Columba and his train.
Within a shout of thine,
Close past this calmly rippled bay,

He must have crossed the waves that shine
From 'lonely Colonsay.'
Then didst thou see him reach
The Isle to which his name has clung,
And didst thou hear upon its beach
His first loud Vespers sung?

II

No ! far too short a line
To sound the depth of distant hours
Since thou wert laid without a sign
Beneath the grass and flowers.
In sands beside the dune,
And near the breaking of the sea,
Thou hear'st the immemorial tune
It ever sang to thee.
Calm in thy lair wild,
With folded limbs in perfect rest,
Thou sleepest like a weanèd child
Upon its mother's breast.

III

The rude old potter's art,
That mouldering lies beside thy feet

Records the beating of some heart
That deemed this tribute meet
To Spirit somewhere fled,
To Spirit-land, it knew not where,
Yet fancied as not really dead,
But needing something there,—
Some memory of its kind,—
Some tie to life as lived below,—
Some still desires of ghostly mind
We can but dimly know.
And so the thoughtful urn
Was moulded out of earth and clay,
And fires were lit to make it burn
Into a thing for aye.
Whate'er it held is gone ;—
Some grain, perhaps, as type of food,
All vanished as the days went on
And as it silent stood :
Yet holding still the tears
That sorrow shed upon thy bier,—
The love, the memory, and the fears
Of those who laid thee here.

IV

Rude as thy burial-stones,
And wild the rocks, the land, the sea
That lie above and round thy bones
And were a home to thee,
Far from the sunny lands
Whence thy wide-wandering fathers came.
And rough the product of their hands,
Thine urn still means the same
That filled the heart of Greek,
On Tuscan or Campanian shore,
Who drew the beauteous forms we seek
In many a hidden store
From tombs beneath the vine,
The olive, and the myrtle-flower,
That speak unburied hopes like thine,
Even in burial hour.
Nor other—the Imperial graves,
Deep-bedded in stupendous pile,
The unmouldering air of Egypt saves
Beside her bounteous Nile.

The same—the same—since man
First laid his brother man in dust.
Let those interpret best who can
This world-wide hope and trust.

April 9, 1893

INHLOBANE,[1] *ZULULAND*

(ON THE DEATH OF HON. RONALD CAMPBELL IN
THE ZULU WAR, MARCH 29, 1879)

OLD rocks that rose above the foam
　Of some primeval sea ;
Fronting the billows as they shaped
　Fair lands that were to be.

Around your proud and lofty line
　The Ocean gleamed again ;
Where now your caves and chasms hold
　Dark swarms of savage men.

[1] Pronounced ' Hlobānè.'

Taking the sunshine and the storm
With fragments strewed below,
Ye watch the passing of the days
As ages come and go.

But never since ye reared your head
In that far southern sky
Saw ye a nobler sight, than when
Ye saw that hero die !

Loved, and with treasures far away,
He bounded up your side ;
In dark retreats he searched the foe,
And on your bosom died.

Ye saw them dig his grassy grave
And lay his gallant head
Where flowers and leaves alone could mark
The slumbers of the dead.

Inhlobane Hill !   Inhlobane Hill !
Thy stones shall wake again
To gentler steps than broke your rest
And leaped to battle then.

She comes, she comes across the wave,
  Who keeps a deathless love !
She comes to bear her cross below
  And see thy crown above.

Dear rocks ! your calm and steadfast line,
  Across the blue of Heaven,
Is graven on her heart for aye,
  Until her rest be given.

And far through time the tongues of men
  From age to age shall tell
How round you once the battle raged,
  And brave young Ronald fell.

THE SILENT FRIEND

DEAR silent friend, whose voiceful eyes
  Have spoken love through many years
Of light and shadow, and the change
  From trembling hope to bitter tears ;

Unchanged, unchanging, ever thou
  Hast shared with me the wakeful hours
In cold and gloom of Northern climes,
  In perfume of Provençal flowers.

And as those Southern suns arose
  In glory o'er the Midland Sea ;
When gentler breathings came to us,
  We knew that they were joy to thee.

Nor didst thou fail, dear faithful one,
  When fainter came the failing breath,
To show in that mute face of thine
  Some strange presentiment of death.

And so thou wouldst not leave him then,
  But laid'st beside his dying feet ;
Thy fair and soft and tender form
  Coiled close around them,—as was meet.

Hail ! creature loves ! In Love Divine
  We see the fountains whence ye came
In bounded natures bounded too,
  ⋅ Yet no false semblance, but the same !

And therefore do I mourn thee dead,
  Remembering all the ways we trod ;
And counting all thy looks of love
  As gleanings in the fields of God.

DANBURY CHASE, ESSEX

ON THE MORNING AFTER THE DEATH OF THOMAS LEGH
CLAUGHTON, FIRST BISHOP OF ST. ALBANS
August, 1892

How still this morning air with mellow lights
  On the rich foliage of those ancient trees !
They've seen, perhaps, a thousand summers pass,
  And many souls more fleeting still than these.

The ' Raven Oak ' that, through the Middle Age,
  On her great branches bore the bird of gloom,
Saw proud Crusaders in their noble rage
  To save from Moslem hands the Saviour's tomb.

And when their armour, pierced in Holy Land,
  Sent its loud clangour to the mourning West,
Her boughs e'en then stretched listening to the sound
  Of chanted benison on knights at rest :

And that tall spire that lifts the village church
High in the air from out its crowning wood
Still points the altar where those prayers were said
And standeth now where even then it stood.

Each later age those stately trees have seen
  Men sport and mourn through all their sun and
    shade :
Heard in the day the hunter's bugle horn,
  And pass at eve the joyous cavalcade.

And little children playing round their feet
  Have lived, and grown, and toiled to agèd head
Resting at noon beneath their shadowing arms,
  Until they saw them numbered with the dead.

And now stag-headed, with some branches bare,
  They still are young as with their younger leaves,
Still living through the little lives of men
  Their seed, their sowing, and their garnered
    sheaves.

But never since those fruitful acorns fell
  In older glades before the Norman's day,
Have they e'er stood around a nobler lord
  Than him who now, again, has passed away.

Farewell, old chase ! for our sad parting ways
  Must leave your dearest shades by us untrod.
Your boughs have sheltered for some blessèd years
  A Prince, and Father, in the Church of God.

LOVE AND SORROW

CAN love still live with love that's lost
In this sad heart so tempest-tossed ?
Yes, love can live with sorrow well,
As they best know who best can tell
How mourning falls on those who mourn,
How near they come whose spirits, torn,
Wear all the weeds that we have worn,—
Who've watched through years the failing powers,
The flickering light of golden hours,
With strength, perhaps, more strong than ours,—
More strong to bear the daily task,
To see the needs too faint to ask,
More strong to own, more brave to speak
The load we bear, the light we seek,

When life that is our very own,
And sounds with ours one music-tone
Goes out and leaves us all alone ;
When what we ask is why we live
Since those are gone whose spirits give
The joys that gilt our earth and sky,
Whose very shadows cannot die,
So soft they dwell in mem'ry's eye :
With such as these can love re-wake,
And hearts re-live which seemed to break.

SONGS OF NATURE AND
THE BIRDS

ON FIRST OBSERVING THE WILLOW
WREN IN MIDWINTER ON THE
PINCIAN HILL, IN ROME, DECEMBER
1842

FAIR summer bird whose very name
    Was ever charm to me,
And is it that this sunny land
    Is winter home to thee?

Then will I feel it nearer home
    And love its beauty more ;
Then will I tread more joyously
    Upon its golden shore ;

F

For thou hast been, thou loved one,
  The joy of early hours,
The first proclaimer, soft one,
  Of spring's returning powers.

Scarce has the yellow primrose seen
  The virgin snowdrop fade,
The wild bee has not 'gun to taste
  The hawthorn's scented shade.

Ere yet the swallow well has reached
  The land with weary wing,
Thrice welcome is thy gentle voice,
  And all its whispers bring.

It is a soft and gentle voice
  That cometh from above,
A song that ever seemed to me
  The very voice of love.

But few do know thee, gentle bird ;
  Few, few have ever seen
The soft-lined mansion thou dost build
  Low in the tufted green.

'Tis there, thy home, that shy retreat,
And there the livelong day
Thou pourest forth unceasingly
Thine oft-repeated lay.

'Tis there, and in that stillest nook
Of some light, budding bower,
How often have I, musing, felt
Thy most mysterious power.

With others I may gladly hear
The Blackbird's music float,
Or pouring forth, the Missel Thrush,
His loud, melodious note.

With brothers and with friends I'll go
Where many a varied voice
Calls from each bush, and tree, and field,
'Rejoice with me, rejoice!'

Yes, other warblers I can love
With love that's all their own,
But when to thee, dear bird, I list,
I must be quite alone.

It is not that the softest sound,—
The rustling of a leaf,—
Will break the whisp'rings of a song
Already all too brief.

It is that if we'd truly feel
The music of the heart,
Or have dim mem'ries softly touched
We must be far apart

From every thought, or sound, or sight,
Save that and that alone
Which hath some mystic power to raise
Dreams of a world unknown.

If ever there's a moment when
All trouble quits my breast,
And leaves it to the sacred balm
Of calmness, love, and rest ;

If e'er association's power,
That wondrous fount of joy,
Almost beguileth me to think
I am again a boy,

If ever to my inmost soul
  I feel I can be glad
With gladness all more deep, because
  It is a little sad,

It is, dear bird, that April day,
  That golden hour of spring,
When first in some quick budding bower
  I hear thee, charmer, sing.

For 'tis the gentlest strain that floats
  Upon the summer air,
There is no room for ruffled thoughts,
  No place for anger there.

It is a soft and gentle voice
  That cometh from above,
A song that ever seemed to me
  The very voice of love.

Then joy, that I have met thee, bird,
  Thrice joy, where'er we roam,
To think, these wintry months away,
  We'll meet again at home,

When the green earth, in every germ,
Feels a reviving power ;
When the yellow primrose gently opes
Its softly scented flower ;

Then joy, that I have met thee, bird,
Thrice joy, where'er we roam,
To think, these wintry months away,
We'll meet again at home.

Now, ask not, stranger, for the name
Of this dear bird of mine,
'Tis one that seldom meets the ear
And 'twould be strange to thine.

It is a small and gentle bird
That shuns the haunts of men ;
And few, who do not seek, have heard
The Lesser Willow Wren.

Rome, 1843

ON A RING-PLOVER

FOUND DEAD IN THE ISLAND OF TIREE, AUGUST, 1884

In a hollow of the dunes
    Its wings were closed in rest,
And the florets of the eyebright
    Stood guard around its breast.

The glorious light and sun
    Were on it where it lay ;
And the sound of ocean murmurs
    Passed o'er it from the bay.

No more its easy pinions
    Would gleam along the sand,
No more, in glancing courses,
    Sweep all the pleasant land.

No more its tuneful whistle
    Would mingle with the surf :
Its busy feet were idle—
    Once nimble on the turf.

No ruffle marred its plumage,
No struggle stretched its head,
It lay in perfect slumber—
The happiest of the dead.

So could I wish that Death
Would make his lair for me
Among the list'ning pastures
And margins of the Sea.

TO THE SAND GROUSE [1]

WHY come ye from the tawny waste
Of the Mongolian plains,
To seek through leagues of stranger air
Our western storms and rains?

Deep in the hollows of that land
Where some rare water gleams,
Ye bask among the flowers and seeds
. Of oleandered streams.

[1] Note XIV., Appendix.

These warm and pebbly colours show
   Your native home to be
In lands that since the raging flood
   Have never seen the sea.

What thought ye of that vaster plain
   Rippling its thousand waves,
Its ships, its freight of living men,
   And all its ' wandering graves ' ?

As wide horizons may have lain
   Under your ranging flight,
Where the great Oxus rolls her sands
   Through quivering fields of light.

Or when from Afghan hills and rocks
   Your arrowy course was hurled
To Ganges from the Pamir steppe,—
   The roof-tree of the world.

But never since your little feet [1]
   Pattered among the stones,
Have ye e'er heard the ocean roar
   Or sing its undertones.

      [1] Note XIV., Appendix.

What mystic impulse, then, has brought
  Your pinions to our West ?
Why thought ye on our scraps of sand
  To find a home or rest ?

Did ye but follow on the march
  That changed the world's rude face,
First scattering broadcast the seeds
  Of our great Aryan race ?

Or was it that ye longed to see,
  Far down the setting flame,
The mighty fountains whence Aral
  And your own Caspian came ?

So we may wing our searching course,
  And guide our lines of flight,
To the great deeps which still have left
  Some little pools of light.

THE DANBURY SWALLOW

WHERE Essex lifts her greenest bower
 And shrines an old chief Pastor's love,¹
Where every leaf on ivied tower
 Hears all day long the brooding dove ;

From out the crowded haunts of life
 Now youth, now age comes seeking there
Peace from the battle and the strife,
 As in some fane of restful prayer.

Uncounted leagues of land and sea
 Bring every summer bird that sings.
Each domesday oak, each clovered lea
 Sees all the glancing of their wings.

The tangled brakes of flowering May
 Pass into garlands rosy red ;
And pools of water hold the day,
 Redoubling glories overhead.

The gleaming fisher of the lake
  Sits watching on her shadowed bough :
Rich turquoise worn for some dear sake
  Set on a dark and lovely brow,

Would pale before the fulgent ray
  That marks the Halcyon's gliding track ;
No mirrored pool beneath her way
  Can throw one half her glories back.

And when she darts upon her prey
  She darts as with a meteor's flight,
Halo'd in showers of diamond spray,
  Blue-flashing in her jewelled light.

And one familiar bird there came,
  That ever sounds her twittering note
By cottage eave and latticed frame,
  From creamy breast, and russet throat.

O'er half the world she finds her way
  To skim each year this English lawn :
Her flight is part of summer day,
  Her wings are busy with the dawn.

She loves no solitary place,
    Nor forest lands, nor moor, nor fen,
She moveth ever in the face
    And round the meadowed homes of men.

One year, for nest, she chose instead
    Of barn, or eave, or raftered door,
The lowly vestibule that led
    Unto a little chapel floor.

All that fair week she carried straws
    And built her fragile house with clay:
No hand enforced the household laws
    That would have stopped her happy way.

Next year she came, and flew around,—
    On one bright morn of perfect calm
Her place was echoing to the sound
    Of children's chanting of a psalm.

She sat entranced, and heard the praise
    That David sang of homing bird;
She heard her name from ancient days,
    And wondered at the gracious word;

Then, waiting till the parting few
    Had passed into the blossomed air,
On to God's altar straight she flew
    And laid her young ones there.

SONG OF THE WATER OUSEL

My home is on the rivers
    That run among the hills,
Through all the sloping valleys,
    Down all the moorland rills.

But clear must be the waters
    As they glide and rush along,
And the woodlands must be lonely
    That hearken to my song.

For there my rhythmic numbers
    Are spread among the stones ;
And the listening water answereth
    In its own low murmuring tones.

And thus we keep such melody
  As the world has never known :
For the river never ceaseth
  To love me as its own.

I love it for the gladness
  It speaketh in my ear,
In all its wayward windings
  Through the cycle of the year.

For in the months of summer,
  When its gentlest currents run
In streams of liquid amber
  All golden in the sun ;

And in the months of winter,
  When every stone is set
In fretted sheets of silver
  That have not melted yet,

We keep our music sounding,
  When other birds are still,
Singing, singing, evermore,
  At our own sweet will.

And when the primrose opens
  Its soft and steady eye,
We then begin our nesting,
  My merry wife and I.

We choose some bank o'erhanging,
  And weave a wondrous dome,
Where she can hear the waters
  And watch the specks of foam

That come from all the breakings,
  Tho' they be miles away,
Yet never miss the eddies
  That bring them by her way.

And all the days of summer
  We dive into its breast ;
And we rout among the pebbles,
  And feed the teeming nest.

And we love to see the shimmer,
  As it rushes overhead,
And we flutter in the noises
  That gurgle from its bed ;

And we scatter little cataracts
    That tumble through our wings,
When we shake the drops from off us
    In a shower of silver rings.

And when we see the movings
    Of little wings that strive,
We never need to teach them
    Or how to swim or dive.

For the music of the river
    Has taught them ere we know,
As came their glossy feathers,
    As came their breasts of snow.

For the pleasant river loved them
    Before they left the nest ;
It laves them in its ripples,
    It bears them on its breast.

And from its banks of blaeberry
    The tall, white stalks of grass
Bend down their plumes to watch us
    And cheer us as we pass.

G

Then we hunt the golden shallows,
  We sound the crystal deeps,
And rest where round some boulder stone
  The languid current sleeps.

At last, a merry family,
  We face the autumn weather,
And spread all up the mountain rills,
  By banks of fern and heather.

SELBORNE

I

How oft in sickness when the languid brain
  Longed for the freshness of a summer wood,
And the tired reason could not bear the strain
  Of ordered thinking which before it stood,
Have I, so longing, just re-read the page
  Of him who wrote of Selborne and its birds,
To whom through years of slow and peaceful age
  Did kindly Nature whisper all her words,

Of spring, and summer, and of autumn sheaves,
   Of strange soft days in winter out of place,
When wakened swallows flew without the leaves,
   And stranger wings had lit in Wolmer chace.

II

Then saw I once again with dreamy eyes
   The great broad shadows close the evening light,
Waking the Dor-hawk to his dewy skies
   And those strange sounds that he doth make at
     night.
I heard from high and fleecy midnight cloud
   How piping cry of 'Great Grey Plover' told
Faint, and more faint, though first it sounded loud,
   Of his quick flight to some far distant Wold.
Then the sweet odours from the 'Hanger' came
   As beechen leaves unfolded tender green,
Till fancy breathed through all my wearied frame
   The air of spring, and all its flowers were seen.

III

And from the tall tree tops one rapid note
   Was shaken out with quivering wings of joy
From upward bill, and from a silver throat,
   As once it rained upon me when a boy.

Again I saw the well-remembered trees
  Whose sunlit foliage seemed with life on fire ;
And whence I heard, new floating on the breeze,
  The song that he first added to the choir
Of warbler birds that now we call our own,—
  Familiar birds that make our woodland ways
So rich in song, so sweet in varied tone,
  And charm the morning of our summer days.
But this shy bird had ever lived on high,
  So far removed from common sight of men,
So like the light and shimmers of the sky,
  They did not know the ' Larger Willow Wren '—
Of three fair sister-birds the fairest one,
  Pale primrose yellows touched its slender form ;
Yet o'er its breast the purest silver won,
  Most fairy bird that fronts the·vernal storm.[1]

IV

And so I turned and turned again the leaves
  Of that old record of a charmèd house,
Saw the weird bats fast dropping from the eaves,
  Or climbed the wheat-stalks with the ' Harvest
                                          [Mouse.'

[1] Note XV., Appendix.

Until my wearied eyes were closed in sleep,
  And woke refreshed as when the night is done,
Saw with fresh health the morning sunbeams sweep,
  And heard at dusk the Portsmouth evening gun.
And so in every English-speaking land
  The name of this dear Selborne stands in light.
For Nature's voice and all her bounteous hand
  Still sings and plays to men through Gilbert White.

KINTYRE

The greenness of the mountain-side
  Was purpled with the heather bloom,
And clouds fast flying far and wide
  Gave happy change of light and gloom.

The shining fields of ocean lay
  With tracts of shadow and of flame,
Whilst lines of surf on sandy bay
  In broken flashes went and came.

The silver-breasted birds that fly
Along the margins of the sea
With rapid wings and piping cry
Sang loud their well-known song to me.

With sudden folding of their wings   .
On shoreward ripples of the strand,
They gathered quick the pearly things
That ocean sendeth to the land.

In clear green streams of racing tide
The snowy Gannet plunged from high,
Dashing the foam on every side,—
An arrow sent by piercing eye.

Then sheering out of middle blue
The wand'ring bird that looks for spoil,[1]
In wheeling circles searched the view
Ranging from crags of windy Moil.[2]

It is the bird whose gallant flight
Was pastime of the Middle Age,
Perched on the arm of mounted knight,
Or held awhile by gentle page.

[1] *Falco Peregrinus.*
[2] The Mull of Kintyre is locally so pronounced.

And when she hovers overhead,
  No wing dare move across the sky ;
All lying close in sign of dread,
  They watch her flight with fearful eye.

But when she moves away again
  And her proud form dissolves in cloud,
The Peewit flaps from moor and glen,
  And joyous Curlew whistles loud.

Then when the sun begins to fall
  Into the great Atlantic bed,
Twin gleams of glory strike on all
  From sea and sky, on harvests led.

It is an open breezy land,
  Well kissed by all the winds that blow,
From east and west, on every hand,
  Fresh seaward clouds drift to and fro.

In ancient days the Viking fleets
  Swept round its shores from hiving north,
Or hauling down their dreadful sheets,
  Ravaged, and bore their plunder forth.

In days more ancient still than those
　When savage intertribal strife
Broke up all lands 'twixt brother foes,
　And cursed them with a murderous life,

The same great sea from Scotia's coast,
　Through rolling waves with breakers curled
Brought to these bays what blesseth most,
　Christ's peaceful message to the world.

For brothers of Columba came
　To 'Alba' in their boats of hide,
And chief of these was Kiaran's [1] name,
　Still whispered round on every tide. [2]

The cave he lived in for retreat,
　The harbour where he sheltered first,
Holding e'er since full many a fleet
　For refuge when the tempests burst,—

All keep his name : twelve hundred years
　Have silenced not its saintly sound,
For still our mourners bear in tears
　Their lost ones to his holy ground.

---

[1] Pronounced 'Keeran.'　　　[2] Note XVI., Appendix.

The altar that he built for prayer,
   Beside Ben Ghuilean's [1] slender rill,
Has left no stone on other there,
   Yet his loved name remaineth still.

For round the spot whereon of yore
   First Christian songs he raised and led,
Slow borne beside St. Kiaran's shore,
   We lay the ashes of our Dead.

Hail, lightsome land! whose hills and slopes
   Front all the suns that rise and set,
Whence distant skies give morning hopes,
   And clouds are seen whilst cloudless yet;

In this fair world, no fairer fields
   Lie quickening to the soul of man :
The smiles and frowns great nature yields
   Are ever round it in the van.

[1] Pronounced 'Ben Gullion,' or 'Ben Goolean.'

OCTOBER

COME burnished autumn with thy wealth of flame,
    And lofty clouds that float in tender blue ;
Come leaves with tints too blended for a name,
    And lakes resoftening lights that come from you ;
Come gentle shadows on the mountains thrown,
    High slopes all roseate at the close of day ;
Come harvest fields by golden stubbles known,
    And garnered sheaves that have been borne away ;
Come perfect stillness, as of sorrow born,
    The passing year as if resigned to die,
Holding reversed her sad and empty horn,
    But loving yet her garlands where they lie.
Come northern wings that fly the icy seas
    Whose crash and roar break down the Polar lands,
Come, fold your pinions where ye meet the breeze
    From southern tides, that bathe our warmer sands.
Come lengthened shadows, and the shortened day,
    And night slow-passing on the ways of space,
With earlier gold that flames itself away
    Into the splendours of her starry face.

Hail changing life that does not speak of death,
But wheels returning from the fount of day ;
Hail Nature's kindly sleep and colder breath
That holds the promise of her distant May.

JANUARY

STERN winter's cold had settled down
On all the mountains round ;
And snow and ice for long had lain,
Holding the lifeless ground.

The spotless hills threw back by day
The sun's low rays of light :
Behind their clear, sharp edges rose
The stars that gemmed the night.

No river ran : in every glen,
On every channelled hill,
The muffled streamlets trickled down,
The waterfalls were still.

The splendour of each morning fell
On every knoll and brae :
Soft shadows traced each least ravine
In tender blues and gray.

In ocean tides, whose rise and fall
Could scarce one pebble fret,
Each gleam of light, each pearly shade
With blended colours met.

The radiance of each daily sun
Died down in after-glow :
Eastward on deep empurpled skies
Flamed the red peaks of snow.

The nights were calm : yet through the air
An arctic breath was felt,
As round the pole-star slowly wheeled
The great Orion's belt.

With startling silence, now and then,
Athwart the skies were hurled,
In fierce combustion-streaks of light,
Some fragments of a world.

Day after day the pageant passed :
  The dawn, the glare, the snow :
Eve after eve the sun went down,
  Columned in lake below.

At last one darker morning broke,
  And softly fell the rain ;
Quickly the wind of western seas
  Breathed a green earth again.

I passed the roots of one old tree
  Where birds had pecked in vain ;
Some spots of white still lingered there,
  Why did they thus remain ?

Nearer I went, and then I saw
  No relics of the frost,
But snowdrop buds that rose to speak
  Of all we love the most,—

Returning life :—the coming year,
  That one great promise kept,—
Remembered in the depths of earth
  Even when Nature slept.

The vast but inorganic world
That recks not years or space,
With cold mechanic roll of suns,
Shines with no living face.

Dread and oppressive is the sweep
Of orbs that rule our clime :
Sweet as the voice of heaven to me,
Pale flower that knew her time.

THE LONELY MOOR

'TWAS on a lonely moor
Where grass and heather grew ;
And distant hills on hills arose,
In fading tints of blue.

The Ocean, too, was seen
To far horizon spread ;
And beauteous ships lay silently
Upon its gleaming bed.

No sound, save that of bird
Or insect in the air,
Or faint-heard bleat of browsing sheep,
Broke the soft stillness there.

The wild bee passing by
From bells of rich perfume
Left fading on the vacant ear
Its deep-toned, happy boom.

I thought upon the haunts—
The crowded haunts of care—
The breathing load of sin and woe
This beauteous world doth bear.

Then wondered how the sky
Could breathe such breath of balm,
And how that vast expanse of sea
Could look so bright and calm.

No voice arose to speak
The festering ills of earth :
All nature lay as restingly
As 'twere her second birth.

Yet 'mongst those soft, blue hills,
    And on that shining sea,
I knew that sickness, pain and death
    Were working constantly.

And far beyond my sight
    In lands I could not see,
I thought how thus fair Nature smiles
    On human misery.

I thought how richly breathes
    Many a scented bower,
Where ruby-birds in sunbeams suck ˙
    The large magnolia flower.

While Afric's scourgèd race
    In fetters bear their toil,
And turn with horrid patience o'er
    The gorgeous-tinted soil.

I thought of that vast land
    Which stretches far and wide,
From where the great South ocean rolls,
    To Egypt's mystic tide.

I thought how large a part
  Of this world's wondrous plan
Lies trodden under naked foot
  Of most degraded man.

A gentle wind arose,
  Which o'er that moor did pass,
It bowed the hare and heather bells,
  It waved the yellow grass ;

And far along the moor
  I marked that softest gale,
Until, methought, it struck the sea
  And filled the joyous sail.

I know not whence it came,
  Nor how its accents fell ;
But the blessed words it spake to me,—
  These, I remember well.

It told me that this sense
  Of beauty and of love,
So thirsty and so grieved on earth,
  Must have its home above ;

H

Where the glorious works of God
Retain His blessing still,
And that most glorious of all,
The human heart and will.

PARAPHRASE FROM METASTASIO

WATERS from the Ocean torn,
The valleys and the mountains lave,
Down rapid rivers calling,
From prisoned fountains falling,
They murmur, and they rave
With passion for the Main,
From whence they came in cloud and rain :
The mighty Sea where they were born,
Far from the hills their drops have worn,
Wherein, when all their wand'rings past,
They long to lose themselves at last.[1]

[1] Note XVII., Appendix.

MISCELLANEOUS

THE 'KING'S COVE' AT UGADALE, KINTYRE

A TALE OF A.D. 1306

MARK well that Cove, for once of yore
　　A boat was seen to beat her way—
　　Coming through storm at close of day
Until her bows had kissed its shore.

Then leaping from the stranded bark,
　　And moving up the copse-wood brae,
　　A Knight was seen to stride away
Until he vanished in the dark.

In one near opening of the wood
　　Where wattled hazels of the time
　　Kept out the rains of windy clime,
Quick stepping to the door he stood.

With courteous yet commanding air
  He asked the way to farther shore :
  He asked for this, he asked no more,
Nor sought for rest or shelter there.

The farmer, though of humble lot,
  Looked at the Knight without surprise,
  Read all his meaning in his eyes,
With noble manners of the Scot.

'Sir Knight, the moorlands you must cross
  Are high and bare,—no friendly trees
  To break the blast of ocean seas,
With swollen streams, and treacherous moss.

My house is poor, but yet the bed
  Of heather and the blazing fire
  Are better than the shrieking choir
Of stormy spirits overhead.'

'Scant time have I,' the Knight replied :
  'You know the troubles of our land,
  And how we're fighting hand to hand
'Gainst England, upon Scotland's side.

Not yet has fortune lent her smiles :
    Until she does I cannot rest :
    And now I go to farthest west
To rouse the Clansmen of the Isles.'

'No boat, Sir Knight, can cross the sea
    Until this storm has passed away ;
    It will have passed by break of day,
Then gladly I'll be guide to thee.'

And so the Scot and Norman Knight,
    On middle floor around the fire,
    Communed and slept in far Kintyre,
Until the morning broke in light.

Then when the peaks of Arran stood
    In cold dark grays against the sky,
    More slowly drifted clouds on high,
More gently swayed the feathery wood.

Up pressed the two, without a stop,
    Through tangled thickets of the hill,
    Breasting its roughness with a will,
Until, ere noon, they reached the top.

Beneath them, the vast ocean lay,
Still heaving with a troubled breast ;
And many a wave with angry crest
Ran foaming on each rock and bay.

To north the scattered clouds had clung
Round lofty Jura's mountain line ;
Whilst silver vapours, thin and fine,
O'er hills of Islay softly hung.

And southward in broad fields of light,
In dazzling shimmers of the sun,
The Antrim coast in dark had won
The nearest hailings of their sight.

And chiefly did the Rathlin Isle
Lie close below them in the clear.
And as the Knight perceived it near
He seemed to greet it with a smile.

Then, resting on broad-hilted blade,
Addressed his comrade of the day :
'Good friend, you've kindly led my way
Now when my fortunes are in shade.

'Tis true thou dost not know my name,
  Nor hinted thou didst care to know.
  With such as thou 'tis always so ;
All noble natures are the same.

Nor did I tell thee all I meant,
  Nor, closely, where I seek to go ;
  To hide, to wander to and fro
Till better days, I now am bent.

My life of venture far and wide
  Has taught me care,—for fear of wile,
  Not from the Scots of leal Argyle,
Yet, still, I lean to caution's side.

I told thee what I seek alone :
  With Edward's claims I know no truce :
  Start not, good friend,—I am The Bruce,
And I shall sit on Scotland's throne.

The levies he has brought a-field
  Will melt like snow in western gale,
  But our proud spirit shall not fail ;
Again I'll raise the sword and shield.

In that lone Isle below us, soon,
 Hid in some hut beside the shore,
 I'll bide my time, come out once more,
And wear the crown I held at Scone.

I tell thee what, in vision seen,
 Upholds me oft in hopeless hour ;
 I know that I shall break the power
That Scotland's curse so long hath been.'

Then bowed the Scot, the son of Kay
 And hailed his comrade as his king :—
 'Would I could wait beneath thy wing,
And lift with thee our standard high.'

'Come thou no farther, friendly man,
 I need no guide to what is seen.
 Tell thou none else where thou hast been
Until thou see'st me in the Van.'

And when the King's re-coming sail
 Had brought him to his great return,
 And when he won at Bannockburn
He well remembered Ugadale.

The lands that bore that sheltering roof,
   Their rocks, their shore, their shingly cove,
   In token of his kingly love,
Were chartered for Mackay's behoof.

For near six hundred years, that land
   Has held his children's children well :
   Still o'er and o'er they love to tell
Of Bruce's footsteps on its strand.

Nor thus alone can they approach
   So nearly to those ancient days ;
   For, full accoutred on the ways,
They're plaided with a noble brooch,

Such as were made in elder time,
   Which Bruce had gifted to their sire,
   With coral, pearl, and crystal fire,
In memory of their morning climb.

And on that spot of parting ways,
   Where Robert Bruce and proud Mackay
   Had stood in light of sea and sky,
A stone still marks heroic days.[1]

[1] Note XVIII., Appendix.

A SUNSET SKY

Sometimes to us in looking up
A wondrous blue is given,
So soft, so calm, divinely pure,
It seems the gate of heaven.
The clouds that gather in the sky
And pass across its face
Are bathed in one ethereal hue,
As of unfathomed space.
And yet they tell us 'tis the dust
Of this poor world of ours
That, floating in the deeps beyond,
So crowns our evening hours.
'Tis well to know it : it may be
Fit emblem to our sight
How earthly things, when lifted hence,
Can be dissolved in light.
Transforming radiance ! Stay with us.
Sad skies are overhead ;
For mournful days and ' dust to dust '
Have left us with the dead.

TEWKESBURY

WHERE Avon and the Severn join
  In one fair tide to reach the sea,
Rises with stately arch and groin
  The minster tower of Tewkesbury.

Built in the grand old Norman days
  When rugged strength in massive stone
Enshrined Belief, and all the ways
  In which men felt and built alone,

It stands unmoved through later times
  Beloved of all this English land ;
And from its bells we hear the chimes
  Rung out by many a mouldered hand.

Beneath its great round-columned floor
  Lies many a knight with arms at rest,
Borne shoulder-high through lofty door
  That oped its chancel to the West.

It holds the warrior bones of those
  Whose fame still rings with loud report.
The mighty men who faced the foes
  Of Crecy and of Agincourt.

Round its grey walls for England's crown
  The Roses clashed in bloody fight,
And now they both, low lying down,
  Sleep in its calm and jewelled light.

And woman's love, enshrined for him
  To whom she gave her virgin heart,
Still holds the colours faint and dim
  That glowed on forms of loveliest art.

The slender shaft, the spreading fan,
  The garland leaves that range o'erhead
Still bower the rich and costly plan
  Of lordly Warwick's burial bed.

Is there no blood that flowing still
  From that old love in living veins,
Can rise to work with heart and will
  To keep its tomb from Time and stains?

Some marble shafts are missing now,
   Some tender pendents from the roof,
The altar stone where prayer and vow
   Were spoken for a soul's behoof.

The world is changed : but Christian faith
   Stands where it stood in days of old.
Old forms are gone ; yet sorrow saith
   All that it then in beauty told.

.

Let reverent hands restore the lost,
   Re-tint the faded colours there,
That those by sorrow tempest-tossed
   May find a kindred rest for prayer.

A FOREST POOL

I PASSED by a pool in a wood,
   Its waters were still and black,
The winds of heaven touched it
   And came with an odour back :

A scent of decay and death,
Of rotting and soddened leaves ;
And I turned to the fields beyond,
With their promise of golden sheaves.
Summer passed : the fields were bare
And the corn was killed with blight,
And the landscape lay in gloom
In a burning and misty light.
I turned to the pool in the wood
From a world that was sad with scars,
For the lilies had blossomed there
And covered its face with stars.
They made it a gorgeous pool,
With radiance rich and rare ;
And the rotting leaves had changed
Into visions of glory there.

A CROSS OF FLOWERS

SHE brought me such a lovely cross
As I had never seen,—
Of water lilies and of moss,
Rare gold and silver sheen.

The radiant petals on it lay,
  Full opened to the skies ;
And yellow anthers hailed the day
  With rich and grateful eyes.

To her pale hand the patient lake
  Its starry treasures gave,
That she might lay them for his sake
  Upon the new-made grave.

' But they will droop, my sister dear,
  Ere they can reach his side.'
' I care not ; but 1 do not fear,'
  The loving child replied.

Yes !   She was right, and I was wrong.
  The true reply she made.
The flowers might die ; but love was strong :—
  Her gathering cannot fade.

ISLAM

ALL plants not planted by My Father's hands,—
Each one of these shall yet be rooted out.
How long, O Lord ? When shall we hear the shout
Of that great victory, and ransomed lands
Be open to Thy light—when see the rout,
In the long sun of that triumphant day,
Of evil legions, as they swarm away
From this fair earth, that would be fair indeed,
But for the noisome growths of evil seed
That choke its furrows ? The Arabian sands
Have sent their raging Prophet forth, and hurled
His bolts of ravage over half the world.
He holds Thy Land. He treads the sacred street
That heard the echoes of Thy blessèd feet.

May, 1892.

CORINTH IN 1843

I

I STOOD at Corinth in the dying lights
Of one fair-born Mediterranean day :
The hills of Athens glimmered in its ray ;
Whilst deepest shadows held Morea's heights.
Soft lines of silver traced out all the bay,—
The old, immortal bay of Salamis.
Ah me ! how ill can we remember this
When all is changed, and odours of decay
Breathe from the myrtled plain where Greek met
    Greek,
And all his Isles came crowding here to seek
The triumph of the Games.   Yet, from the ground
Lone columns rise that listened to the sound
Of murmurous feet, the tumult, and the cries,
The shouts of Victory that rent the skies.

May 30, 1892

1

II

How full this speechless sadness of the past,
This sense that every young and noble brow
That rose and fronted men is mouldered now
By suns and rains and storms,—its atoms cast
In lower forms, each meaner than the last.
Alas ! shall all our strivings thus be lost
Indeed ?   Shall all our gettings, tempest-tost,
Be scattered, like the dust before the blast
Of all-devouring Time ?   Shall nothing stand—
Not the great stars, nor seas, nor solid land ?
I called again, ' Is nothing worth these cries
Of high endeavour, and of great emprise ? '
The answer came,—' No wrestler for the Truth
Shall lose the laurels of immortal youth ! '

Danbury : *June* 2, 1892

TO THE SONNET

Avon's great Prophet has revealed thy power
To twine all tendrils of the human heart,
And hold its sweetness through melodious art
Within the leafage of thy slender bower.
Green Rydal's Bard recounts thy glorious part
In Poet's song ; recalls the tender voice
That took thee with a long and loving choice
To tell their sorrows; and indeed we start
To hear the roll-call of the names that lie
With thee,—since thou wert born in Italy :—
Immortal names ; and as we hear the calls
They sound to us from out thy narrow walls,
We bend our ears, and almost seem to see
The mighty Dead who loved to speak in thee.

London : *May* 21, 1892

———————

WALMER CASTLE

July 16-17, 1893

AND was it here he died who shook the power
  Of Europe's tyrant in his days of pride?
Who taught the peoples to await the hour
  That did, through him, both stay and stem the tide

Till roused to hope, with burning sense of wrong,
  The flocking nations to his standard came,
And one who seemed so ruthless and so strong
  Broke to his onset, and fell down in flame?

And was it here he lived in peaceful days—
  In this old Fort that held his native land,
And watched with cannon all the southern bays
  That fronted France, and lay to foeman's hand?

Upon these strong old bastioned walls he paced,
  Beside the guns that woke no thunder then;
Where pilèd balls, by seedling flowrets graced,
  Unhandled, showed the changeful ways of men.

Changeful, and yet unchanged, for well he knew
  Those winding tendrils round the cannon balls
Still flowered and fruited in the Lines he drew
  Round Torres Vedras, and fair Lisbon's walls.

And so through years of his most honoured age
  He knew that peace was conquered still by arms,
Wrote and re-wrote on many a warning page
  How, only, England could be kept from harms.

Nor feared he to retreat, as once before,
  When civil strife had laid too hard a strain ;
Peace above all within this Island shore
  He strove to make, nor did he strive in vain.

And therefore did he bear with calm reserve
  The loud reproaches that on him were cast,
Knowing that those who really faithful serve
  Will hold the love of nations at the last.

Nor did he think or care for human thanks
  Save as they came with sense of duty done ;
In civil strife he fought as in the ranks,
  Command obeyed,—the only spoils he won.

And here for years of tribute and of praise
  He held the post of Warden, as was meet,
Beside the Roads where saw his younger days
  The glorious flag of Nelson and his fleet.

For thanks had come at length in vast acclaim
  From all his country's fields, and towers, and towns
Holding in love the letters of his name,
  Till here he died—still looking on ' The Downs.'

TO WILLIAM PITT

I HEARD the noises of outrageous seas,
And angry breakers leaping on the strand,
And sounds more deep and dreadful still than these,
As rifts and quakings shook the solid land.
Then saw I one majestic front, whose form
Rose like a mountain peak above the storm.
Around his head all lightnings harmless played.
Men looked and felt they could not be dismayed,
So firm he stood.   In clarion tones he spoke,—

Calling to arms until the morning broke.

And when it broke, the deluge past,

The storm, the ravage, and the shattered throne,

Then in the calmness of our peace at last

He dwells in memory—silent and alone.

APPENDIX

———◦◦———

Note I

'OUR largest units die.'—I have found that this expression is not universally understood by those unfamiliar with the language of popular astronomy. Until very recently the distances of the heavenly bodies have been almost universally expressed in numbers referring to the unit of a British mile. The result, of course, is that those distances are made to appear very much more inconceivable than they really are. It is in the numbers of a unit ridiculously inadequate, not in the absolute distance in itself that, very often, the inconceivability lies. The same inconceivability would be the result of measuring our earthly distances by such a unit, for example, as one-tenth of an inch. Upon such a basis of computation the distance between St. Petersburg and Naples might well appear to be inconceivable. The diameter of our globe—or its circumference—treated as a unit in the measurements of celestial distances, would reduce very much the difficulties of conception respecting them. Both of these magnitudes are now easily conceived of as a unit. The length of our planetary orbit would be still more adequate, but it is hardly enough familiar. Yet even the largest of these units 'die' in the immensities of sidereal astronomy when they are employed to represent in figures the distances of the stars. Quite recently it has become common to run into the opposite extreme, and to make use, or at least to pretend to make use, of a new unit which is in itself wholly inconceivable—namely, the distance which is traversed by light in one year. We have only to try to compute what this distance is, at the velocity of 186 thousand miles in every second, in order to be convinced that such a unit is practically no aid whatever to our minds in the difficulties of grasping the greatness of sidereal space. Yet even this inconceivable unit is found to need large multipliers to represent, even conventionally, some of the stellar distances.

NOTE II

'At least, perhaps.'—These words may seem too merely conjectural for the adequate description of the indications of intimate connection which have been recently detected between the luminiferous ether and the phenomena of electric and magnetic force, with which, again, the force of gravitation stands in some close but unknown relation. I am incompetent to express any opinion on the subject. But, metaphysically, it has always seemed to me that, as Newton said, 'action at a distance' is inconceivable and impossible; and if this be true, gravitation must be due to the action of some medium in which all ponderable matter moves.

NOTE III

This stanza refers to, and describes, the most nearly exceptional, and in this sense the most mysterious, of all the organic structures which biological science has been called upon to investigate and explain—namely, the electric organs in certain fishes. It has always appeared to me that they have the very highest interest and value in philosophy. Darwin said of them, 'It is impossible to conceive by what steps these wondrous organs have been produced.'[1] This, in a sense, is true. But it is not impossible at all, on the contrary it is easy and certain, to perceive that certain suggested 'steps' cannot possibly be the secret of their production. 'Natural selection' cannot possibly have been the process, for the obvious reason that the selective effects of use cannot have come into operation before functional use itself had begun to be. Since the days of Darwin a whole literature has accumulated on the intimate structure of the electric organs, and every investigation goes to prove more and more clearly that the steps of development have been taken through a long course of time, during which functional use lay, as yet, in a distant future. In some fishes they exist already largely developed, and yet not hitherto functionally used. The conclusion is inevitable that the steps of evolution have been taken under the guidance and foreknowledge of Mind, exhibiting all its special attributes as we know and recognise them in ourselves. So conclusive is this argument, and so crucial is the case of the electric organs as an exhibition of it, that Dr. G. J. Romanes has been obliged to admit it, and to escape from its fire by retreating into an assertion that these organs are almost a solitary exception in the whole of nature : 'So that,' he says, 'if there were many other cases of the like kind to be met with in nature, I should myself at once allow that the theory of natural selection would

[1] *Origin of Species*, 1st edit., ch. vi. p. 192.

have to be discarded.'[1] But this is a complete surrender, because nothing is more generally admitted in biological science than that all structures which are apparently exceptional are merely specialised developments of germinal elements which are common to all organic structures; and in this particular case the same conclusion has been established by microscopic dissection, proving the gradual conversion of the ordinary fibre of muscle, and the ordinary structure of nervous tissue, into the specialised apparatus of a battery. The whole theory of development, or evolution, is not only consistent with, but is full of, this principle or law. Not only sometimes, but, so far as we can see, always, germs have included potentially all the elements of structure which could only become of functional use in a future more or less deferred. All nature is thus full of prophecy.

NOTE IV

In this stanza the same argument is applied to other cases in the organic world, and especially to the development of flying animals.

NOTE V

This stanza refers to another very special case—that of the Gall Flies (Cynipidæ, &c.), with which I have dealt at some length in the ' Unity of Nature.'[2] The cycle of operations—long and complicated—through which very special ends are attained in this case (through the combined and adapted work of animal and vegetable life) is perhaps one of the most striking and wonderful in nature. It is a cycle of operations involving at every step preparation for the future in a long series of results.

[1] *Darwin and after Darwin*, p. 373.
[2] *Unity of Nature*, pp. 68-75. John Murray, London.

Note VI

These lines refer to the case of the 'Megapodes,' a family of birds peculiar to, but extending over all, the islands of the Eastern Archipelago from the Philippines to Australia. Unlike any other bird, they neither themselves incubate nor hatch their own eggs, nor do they, like the Cuckoos and some other species, trust them to a foster-parentage. But they lay their eggs in hatching mounds of sand, gravel, and vegetable matter, collected or scraped together by their own feet, and so composed and constructed that the requisite heat is supplied by fermentation. The eggs are so large as to give a special amount of room for the perfect development of the chick before exclusion takes place. The young bird is thus born in a condition to scratch its own way out of the mound, and to run, and fly, and enter at once upon its independent individual life. Although there is some analogy between this and the hatching of reptile eggs which are deposited in the sand, there is this essential difference—that the mounds of the Megapode birds seem to be generally, if not always, constructed in the densest shade available, so that the heat depended upon is not that simply of the sun, but is that due to fermentation in the materials gathered for that purpose by the parent birds. Here we have again a case of genuine inspiration—of intuitive perceptions not reached by reason, but the gift of instinctive powers.

Note VII

These lines, as will be seen, are paraphrased from many verses in the 49th chapter of the Prophet Isaiah. The 'newer criticism' has not yet attempted to bring down the date of these writings to a time within several centuries of the Christian era.

Neither can any theory of interpretation explain away the over-whelming extent of correspondence between the vision and its accomplishment in the history and in the triumphs of Christianity. The splendour, and the pathos, and the power, and yet the mystery of the language breathe the very air and spirit of in-spiration ; and when we remember the intense tribal pride of the Jews, and the contempt which they nursed in their minds against all the Gentile races, it is impossible to connect the idea of such a vision with any natural product of Hebrew preconcep-tions. All these preconceptions were opposed to such an ending to God's dealings with the world, and the almost invidious comparison which the Prophet draws between the littleness of the narrow country which had been so long iden-tified with all the glories of Israel, and the vast spiritual dominion which was to cover the most distant regions of the earth, with its farthest islands, is a vision of long subsequent events which involves all the elements of that which is now so much questioned—namely, purely predictive prophecy in the very highest, and yet in the most unquestionable form.

NOTE VIII

' Unseen, within, he moves, inspires.'—The idea that the old ' argument from design,' even in the form which it took in the hands of Paley, is tainted with one essential error—namely, that of conceiving of the Deity as a great mechanic, or artificer, making things as we make them, by working on matter as it were from the outside—is an idea which is itself founded on a complete confusion as to the meaning of the word ' design.' That word has no necessary reference whatever to any par-ticular kinds of process by which mental purpose may be effected. These may be absolutely various, different, or even opposite in their nature. But the thing in which design or purpose consists remains wholly unaffected by any amount of difference in the means, or in the methods, which may be employed for the attainment of its aims. This is a distinction which cannot be too much insisted on, if we are to reconcile the irresistible convictions of our own minds in their recognition of design in nature, with the equally obvious fact that the methods of operation are entirely different, pointing as they do to that immanence and ubiquity of Supreme Power which is the highest conclusion alike of philosophy and of faith.

NOTE IX

I find that the image presented in these lines does not explain itself easily to those who have never seen our West Highland lochs in the herring fishery season. Arms of the sea such as Loch Fyne, or Loch Hourn, wind their way among the mountains so far that some of their deepest parts may be thirty or forty miles from anything like the open ocean. Their shores are full of land-locked creeks and bays—some of them wooded to the beach ; and in these creeks the boats rest in groups at anchor during the day, with fires lighted for cooking purposes, and with wreaths and coils of smoke rising among the hills, all reflected in the glassy water. It has often struck me as an impressive thought that the surface on which these boats thus rested was one continuous surface over the whole globe, and that the farthest and widest spaces of the Atlantic and Pacific oceans were equally open and accessible from these creeks although nothing could be seen from them beyond a few encircling rocks and a few overhanging trees of birch, or ash, or pine.

NOTE X

Tennyson, on my last visit to him, not long before his death, turned in his garden walk, and said emphatically, ' I hate scorn.' Those who know the ' Idylls ' well will recollect the passage in Guinevere where this sentiment is nobly expressed :

> For in those days
> No knight of Arthur's noblest dealt in scorn ;
> But, if a man were halt or hunch'd, in him
> By those whom God had made full-limb'd and tall,
> Scorn was allow'd as part of his defect,
> And he was answer'd softly by the King
> And all his Table.

The same feeling is expressed in his lines on 'The Poet,' where the ' scorn of scorn ' comes among the very first of the highest endowments, there described.

NOTE XI

These verses were written under the impulse of a very strong feeling that all but a very few of the obituary poems which appeared in the press on the Laureate's death failed deplorably in even indicating the lofty religious and ethical teaching of his writings. From personal converse with him during a long course of years I know how strongly he clung to the great verities of Christian belief—to a degree all the more striking because of that aloofness which he always maintained as regarded the ordinary questions of mere theological controversy.

NOTE XII

Some of my readers will remember the beautiful lines addressed to this Duchess of Sutherland by one who had much occasion, in a time of adversity, to feel that characteristic of her lofty nature which I have referred to here. These lines were written by the Hon. Mrs. Norton in 1840 :—

> For easy are the alms the rich man spares
> To sons of genius, by misfortune bent,
> But thou gav'st *me*, what woman seldom dares,
> Belief—in spite of many a cold dissent—
> When, slandered and maligned, I stood apart
> From those whose bounded power hath wrung, not
> crushed, my heart.[1]

Note XIII

Mrs. Beecher Stowe and Garibaldi were both received by he Duchess at Stafford House, on their first visits to England, with a greeting which they both deeply felt, and which the public did not fail to appreciate.

Note XIV

The Sand Grouse (*Syrrhaptes paradoxus*) inhabits the deserts of Central Asia from the Caspian to the Wall of China. It is a bird of immense powers of flight, ranging for thousands of miles in vast flocks over the great spaces which afford it food and water. In 1863 some strange migratory impulse brought numerous coveys to Western Europe, and to the British Isles. In a more recent year a similar impulse brought them here again in much greater numbers, and they attracted such attention that an Act of Parliament was passed for their protection, in the somewhat hopeless expectation that they might settle permanently

---

[1] *The Dream, &c.*, Dedication, p. viii.

K

in the British Isles.   The plumage is very beautiful, closely re-
sembling the colours of the desert.

The feet are very peculiar, having only three toes, and
these small, and glued together close up to the claws.

NOTE XV

Gilbert White was the first discoverer of the larger Willow
Wren—now more commonly known as the 'Wood Wren,' or
(more locally) as the 'Beech Wren' (*Sylvia sylvicola*, Yarrell).
This discovery was communicated to Thomas Pennant in a
letter dated August 17, 1768, in which he says that he had then
before him all the three species of Willow Wren, and describes
them severally, both as to plumage and as to song.   'Shivering
a little with its wings when it sings,' are the words in which he
refers to the Wood Wren—a peculiarity to which I have alluded
in these verses.   The 'Harvest Mouse' was another discovery
of this eminent naturalist.

NOTE XVI

In these two verses 'Scotia' refers to Ireland, as it always
did in those early centuries; whilst the land now called Scotland is named 'Alba,' the appellation universally given to it
by the Irish missionaries of the Columban age.

NOTE XVII

This passage is taken from the 'Artaserse' (Act iii. sc. 1)
of Metastasio—lines to which my attention was called by my

friend Canon Knox Little. But the beauty, point, and delicacy of the Italian is unapproachable in English.

> L' onda dal mar divisa
> Bagna la valle e 'l monte ;
> Va passaggiera
> In fiume,
> Va prigioniera
> In fonte,
> Mormora sempre, e geme
> Fin che non torna al mare,
> Al mar, dove ella nacque,
> Dove acquistò gli umori,
> Dove da lunghi errori
> Spera di riposar.

NOTE XVIII

This poem is a true story. It is embalmed in all the traditions of the people, and the brooch given to his ancestor, as also the lands, by Robert the Bruce, are still in the worthy possession of my old friend Hector Macneal, of Ugadale.

PRINTED BY
SPOTTISWOODE AND CO., NEW-STREET SQUARE
LONDON